CHIP CARVED
Christmas Ornaments

46 Patterns with
Infinite Variations

By Bruce and Judy Nicholas

A *Woodcarving Illustrated* book
www.WoodcarvingIllustrated.com

FOX CHAPEL
PUBLISHING

Acknowledgments

It is safe to say that not much happens in a vacuum. This book is no exception. During my several decades of chip carving, I have had the honor to know some of the nicest, warmest, and most sharing people on this planet. Their influence continues to be a part of my work today, and will continue to be throughout my career.

To Wayne Barton, teacher, mentor, and friend, who nearly single handedly saved chip carving from becoming a lost art form.

To Mindy Kinsey, Carly Glasmyre, and every one of the good folks at Fox Chapel Publishing, who are providing artists of many types with a professional stage on which to display their works.

To learn more about the other great books from Fox Chapel Publishing, or to find a retailer near you, call toll-free 800-457-9112 or visit us at *www.FoxChapelPublishing.com*.

Note to Authors: We are always looking for talented authors to write new books. Please send a brief letter describing your idea to Acquisition Editor, 1970 Broad Street, East Petersburg, PA 17520.

Printed in the United States of America
First printing

About the Authors

Bruce Nicholas

A long-time woodworker, Bruce discovered chip carving in the mid-1980s. A chance meeting with Wayne Barton at a woodworking show opened the door to an entirely new facet of working with wood.

Bruce began teaching chip carving in the early 1990s. Since then, he has taught hundreds of students in beginning and advanced classes. Teaching led to supplying chip-carving tools and project supplies. Since those early days, Nicholas Woodcarving Ltd. has shipped supplies throughout the United States and seven foreign countries.

Most important, Bruce continues to build and carve items on a regular basis, both for show competitions and for the many customers who now enjoy owning his carvings.

Judy Nicholas

Judy's interest in painting began in the early 1980s. After taking a variety of classes, she focused her efforts on folk painting. Over the years she has studied and painted American, Swiss, and Norwegian styles of folk art. She quickly saw the potential for combining her painting skills with Bruce's chip carving. Dissatisfied with results from conventional paints, she developed her own method of using water-soluble wax crayons.

Judy is also responsible for the finish applied to the unpainted carvings. Today her work blends seamlessly with Bruce's carving to create a line of unique and colorful pieces.

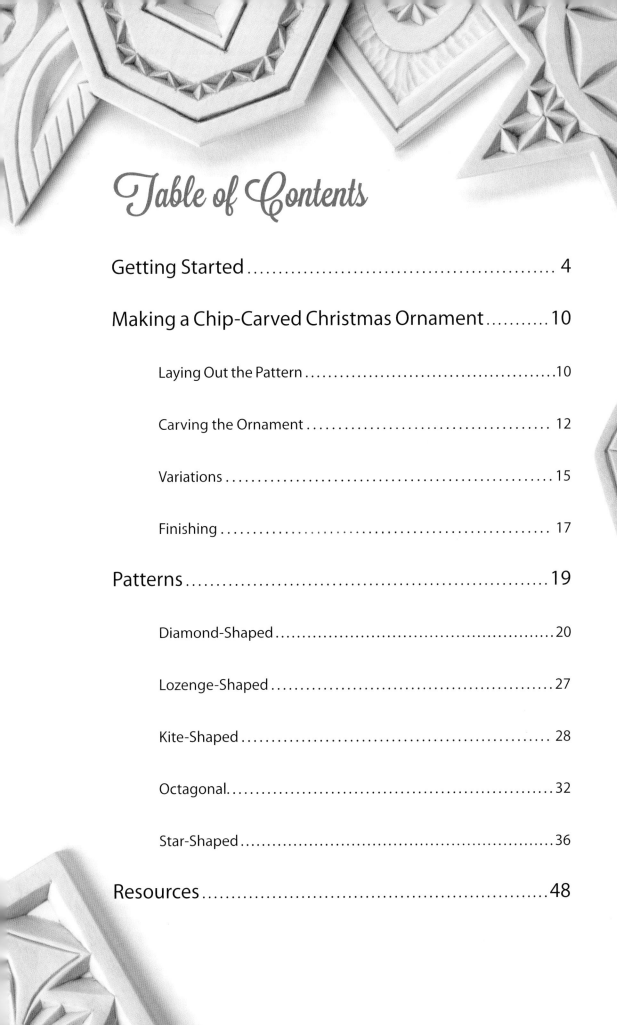

Table of Contents

Getting Started

Every year, woodcarvers create thousands of Christmas tree ornaments to sell, give, or donate to charity. I am one of these woodcarvers, and my chosen method for creating ornaments is chip carving. Chip carving involves removing two-, three-, four- (or even more!) sided chips from wood. I use specific hand positions to cut all of the chips at a 65° angle, as chips cut at this angle produce shadows that ultimately create the design.

This book covers everything you need to know to start chip carving—the correct hand positions, carving an ornament, adding color with water-soluble wax crayons, and more! It includes a step-by-step project, 46 patterns you can start carving immediately, and information on creating custom patterns.

Carving Tools

Knives

I use Wayne Barton Premier chip-carving knives for all of my carvings. I use the cutting knife to carve all of the chips, and I use the stab knife sparingly to add cut detail marks to accent the designs. I use just one cutting knife to increase the accuracy of my cuts. To be a successful chip carver, you need to know your knife so well that you can sense where the point of the knife is without seeing it. When you know this, you'll be able to apply the correct amount of pressure to seat the tip of the blade at the center of the chip to make a perfect chip. This requires practice to develop the hand-eye coordination, and changing from one knife to another means you need to start the learning process all over again.

Sharpening Tools

A good chip carving also requires sharp tools. I use Wayne Barton's ceramic stones; gray for sharpening and white to polish the blade. Ceramic stones come perfectly flat and stay that way even with extended use. When sharpening chip-carving knives, you can easily wear a cup or groove in traditional sharpening stones. This cup or groove will round the cutting edge as you sharpen, preventing you from getting a sharp edge and resulting in poorly cut chips. I avoid buffing wheels and soft strops for the same reason. While the white stone gives me a polished enough edge, if you still want to strop, use a thin strop with a solid backing, such as those made by John Dunkle.

Measuring and Marking Tools

To transfer a pattern quickly and easily to a blank, trace the pattern onto the blank using Saral™ Transfer paper. Saral doesn't smear or penetrate the pores of the wood, which makes it easier to clean up than carbon paper or graphite paper (both of which can ruin a carving if you aren't careful).

If you want a more accurate transfer, use drafting tools to draw the design right on the blank. I suggest using a .5mm mechanical pencil with B lead, which gives you a dark narrow line without denting the blank. I draw most patterns with a 12" T-square marked with both imperial (inches) and millimeters; I use a flexible ruler marked with metric and imperial increments, as well. Use a compass with a thumbwheel adjustment and B lead or a circle guide to draw circles. A good eraser and 220-grit sandpaper make the process easier, and an angle guide, such as a Goniometer or woodworker's bevel gauge, makes duplicating angles effortless.

Advanced Tools

I use a ⅛" (3mm) mini gouge to carve down, or relieve, areas on some ornaments. After relieving, I use a nail set to add texture to the relieved areas.

Hand Positions

Cutting Knife

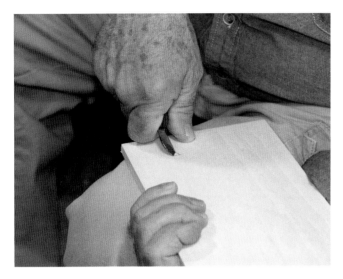

Position 1: Hold the knife with the blade in line with your arm. Position your thumb, knuckle, and the tip of the blade in contact with the wood to create a tripod. The solid tripod grip allows you to maintain the proper angle and keep the cuts consistent. As you carve the chips, move the knife and your hand as a single unit. Keep the hand holding the blank on the blunt side of the knife.

Position 2: Rotate the knife 180° so your thumb is on the spine (blunt side) of the blade. Position your knuckles and the blade tip on the wood. Use Position 1 to carve the first side of the triangle. Turn the blank and shift the knife to Position 2 to cut the second side of the triangle. Then, switch back to Position 1 to cut the third side of the triangle without turning the blank.

Stab Knife

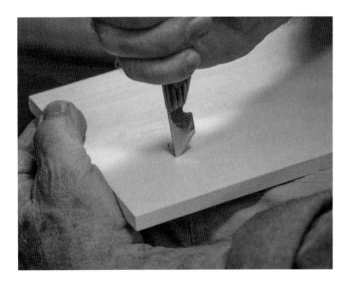

Grip the handle in your fist, wrapping your fingers around the handle. Position your thumb on the end of the handle. Hold the knife perpendicular to the blank, press the blade into the wood, and roll the handle back toward your body.

Sharpening

The sharpening process is similar for the cutting knife and the stab knife. Both require you to hold the sharpening stone securely; any rocking of the knife or stone while sharpening will round the cutting edge.

For the cutting knife, hold the blade flat against the gray stone. Carefully lift the back, or spine, slightly (enough to slip a dime between the stone and the blade). Move the knife back and forth across the stone somewhere between 10 and 20 times. Flip the knife over and repeat the process for the other side. Rub your finger down the bevel toward the cutting edge, feeling for a burr (or wire edge). The goal is to have an even wire edge the length of the cutting edge. Hold the knife at the same angle, but reduce the pressure to remove the wire edge. Repeat the process with the white stone to polish the blade.

Most stab knives come with a bevel ground by the toolmaker. To sharpen the stab knife, hold the tool angled so that the bevel is flat on the stone. The rest of the sharpening process is identical to sharpening the cutting knife.

Wood Selection

For these ornaments, I suggest using basswood harvested specifically for woodcarving. Look for the creamy white variety; the lighter the color of the wood, the easier it is to carve.

As you select and carve basswood, consider the moisture content. If the basswood crumbles against the knife and you know the knife is sharp, the wood is too dry. To remedy this, fill a spray bottle with a 50/50 mix of water and rubbing alcohol. Spray the mix on both sides of the blank and allow it to soak in for a few minutes. You'll notice the difference right away.

Carving Safety

Properly done, chip carving is a very safe form of woodcarving. To carve deep chips, make several small cuts rather than trying to carve the chip in one cut. This technique preserves your control and reduces the risk of injury. It can be tempting to try to cut large or deep chips in one cut, but whenever you apply a lot of pressure, your control is reduced and there's a chance the knife will slip or the blank will split. This puts your hand holding the blank at risk. It's always a good rule of thumb to position this hand toward the blunt side (spine) of the knife. A simple carving jig also increases your safety.

Making a Carving Jig

Cut a piece of ⅜" (10mm)-thick basswood to 6" by 12" (152mm by 305mm), and screw or nail two ½" by ½" by 3" (13mm by 13mm by 76mm) cleats to the plywood at a 90° angle, with a small gap at the point to allow the chips to escape. Hold the blank against the cleats as you carve to keep the sharp blade away from the hand holding the blank.

Holding a small, thin blank safely can be a challenge. Use this jig to hold the blank as you carve.

Basic Cuts

This section shows you how to remove the chips that make up the ornaments in this book. The main chips are line, two-sided, three-sided triangular (large and small), four-sided rectangular, and four-sided chevron-shaped. In our designs, we often repeat the same chip to create borders and shapes, and also combine different chips to make shapes.

The cutting order is really important when we use repeating chips as borders and to make shapes, so we note the correct order for removing chips for the three-sided triangular chips in a shape and four-sided rectangular chip. Stop cuts are not usually used in chip carving, except when carving larger pierced chips. When carving adjacent chips, make the first cut of the second chip with the knife blade pointing away from the first chip. This prevents the blade from exerting too much pressure and damaging the side wall (or ridge) between the chips. This also determines the sequence for removing the chips.

Note: All cuts are made with the knife in the Position 1 (see page 5) unless stated otherwise.

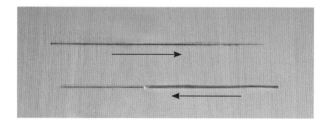

Line Chip

A line is carved as a two-sided chip.

(1) Draw a line. Insert the tip of the knife into the blank slightly to the right of the line. Angle the tip of the blade so it is centered under the line. With the knife and hand moving as a unit, make the first cut. Use the hand holding the blank to turn it slightly to maintain an even distance from the line.

(2) Turn the blank 180° and repeat this process to cut the other side of the line. Remove the chip.

Two-Sided Chip

(1) Turn the blank so the curved side of the chip faces your right. Place the tip of the knife at the far end of the chip. Raise the knife handle so the blade enters the blank vertically, keeping a 65° angle. This position will make the smoothest side wall possible. Make the cut in one continuous movement, starting shallow, moving deeper toward the center, and then ending shallowly to complete the cut.

(2) Turn the blank 180° and cut the straight side of the chip. The depth of the knife will vary just as it did on the first cut. Remove the chip.

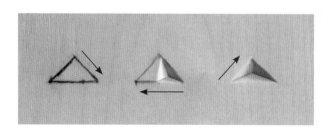

Three-Sided Triangular (Large) Chip

(1) Place the tip of the knife at one corner of the triangle. Insert the knife into the wood until the cutting edge reaches the opposite corner.

(2) Repeat on the other two sides, and remove the chip.

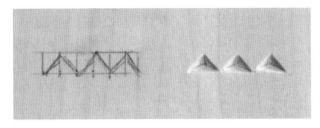

Three-Sided Triangular Chips in a Shape

When a pattern has three-sided triangular chips in a square or circular shape, the cutting order is critical. In order to keep the chips' ridges intact, you must end on a chip that has one side aligned with the grain.

(1) First, establish the grain direction, and then choose a triangle that has one side aligned with the grain. Follow the process to cut a three-sided triangular chip to remove the first chip.

(2) Remove the second chip. This chip should be on the opposite side of the first chip. Make the first cut with the knife pointing away from the first chip.

(3) Continue to remove chips until one remains. This uncarved chip has existing chips on both sides, and it is important to keep the existing chips' ridges intact. Because you followed the correct cutting order, this uncarved chip has one side aligned with the grain. Now you can remove the chip easily and without damaging any of the surrounding ridges.

Three-Sided Triangular (Small) Chip

Small three-sided triangular chips are often strung together to create a border or a design. To make these cuts quickly and easily, you'll use both Position 1 and Position 2 (see page 5).

(1) Place the tip of the blade at the top of the triangle. Insert the knife into the wood until the cutting edge reaches the bottom corner.

(2) Rotate the board 180º and move the knife to Position 2. Place the tip of the knife at the top of the triangle and cut the second side.

(3) Without moving the blank, return the knife to the Position 1 and cut the base of the triangle. Remove the chip.

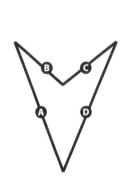

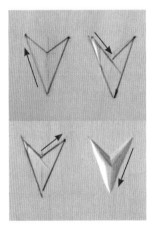

Four-Sided Chevron-Shaped Chip

(1) Place the tip of the blade at the point of the triangle and cut toward the wide end. The depth of the cut will vary according to the width of the chip.

(2) Turn the blank 180º and cut B. Cut toward the center of the chevron, and continue cutting past the center point until the cutting edge of the knife is about 1⁄32" (1mm) from D.

(3) Rotate the blank 180º and place the tip of the blade approximately 1⁄32" (1mm) from A and in line with C. Cut toward the wide end.

(4) Rotate the blank 180º and cut D. Remove the chip.

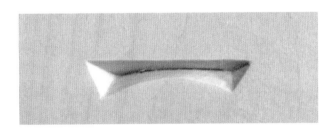

Four-Sided Rectangular Chip

For all of these cuts, angle the blade toward the centerline of the chip. Begin on one side of the rectangle and continue around the chip. Remove the chip after you've made the last cut. As when you cut the triangular chips in a shape, when you use four-sided rectangular chips as a border, make sure to start and end on a rectangular chip that has a side aligned with the grain.

Making a Chip-Carved Christmas Ornament

This pattern is a great introduction to chip carving an ornament. Generalize what you learn here to carve the other patterns in this book. The pattern for this project is on the first page of the Pattern section (page 19).

Materials & Tools

MATERIALS:

Basswood blank, ¼" (6mm) thick: 3" x 3" (76mm x 76mm)

.5MM mechanical pencil with B-lead

Saral Transfer paper

Eraser

Sandpaper

Clear spray finish

Water-soluble wax crayons

Flow medium

TOOLS:

Chip-carving knife

Carving jig

Paintbrushes

12" T-Square

Laying Out the Pattern

Cut the blank to size and sand it with progressively finer grits of sandpaper up to 220 grit. Trace the pattern onto the blank using Saral Transfer paper, or follow the instructions at right to draw the pattern on the blank.

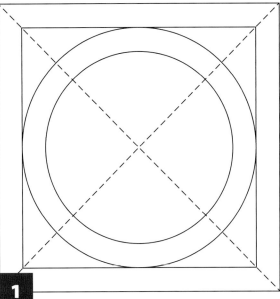

1 **Draw the borders**. Connect the opposite corners of the blank with diagonal dotted lines. Measure ¼" (6mm) from each edge to establish the outer border. Then, draw a ring inside the outer border. Use a compass to draw a 2½" (64mm)-diameter circle and then a 2" (52mm)-diameter circle inside the first.

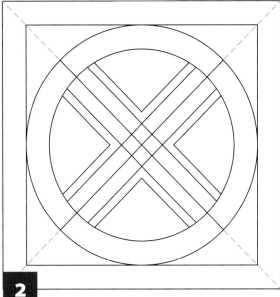

2 **Draw the center design.** Connect the dotted diagonal lines that cross inside the ring. These make the centerlines of an X design. Then, measure 5⁄32" (4mm) from each centerline and draw two lines on either side. This will create a larger X. Draw a border on the outside of each side of the X; this marks the edges of the piercings around the X.

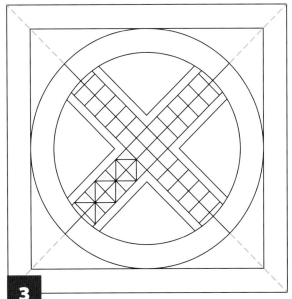

3 **Draw the crosses.** Split the X into equal segments to make small squares. Four of these small squares create the crosses that make up the X. To establish the crosses, draw diagonal lines that cross through the center of the four squares. If desired, dot the chips that will be removed (shown above as blue dots).

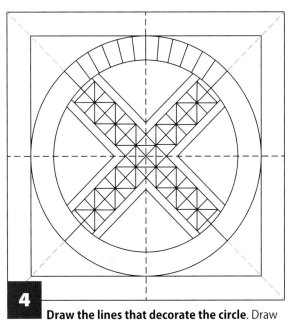

4 **Draw the lines that decorate the circle**. Draw two perpendicular lines that cross in the center of the blank. These lines paired with the diagonal lines drawn in Step 1 split the ring into eight equal parts. Divide each part into six equal segments by eye.

Note: Finished pattern is on page 19.

Carving the Ornament

1 **Carve the largest chips first.** These chips, which are pierced in this ornament, are larger versions of the basic three-sided chips (see page 8). Make the three standard cuts, and then repeat the process until all three cuts pierce through the back and free the chip. Don't try to carve through the chip in one pass; I usually carve halfway through in the first pass. Take care as you cut the sides of the triangle that run with the grain of the wood; applying too much pressure could cause the blank to split. Use this process to cut the other three corner chips.

2 **Refine the pierced openings.** Turn the blank over and determine which pierced opening's side wall is closest to the edge of the blank. Use a T-Square to draw lines around the blank based on this opening. Shave wood off the side walls using these lines as a guide to adjust all the openings to an equal size.

3 **Carve the curved edges of the large chips in the middle of the ornament.** Raise the knife handle until only the tip of the knife is in the wood. This will allow the knife to turn tighter corners without leaving marks on the side wall of the chip. Repeat the cuts while maintaining the same angle to pierce through the ornament. Carve all four large middle chips.

4 **Refine the large middle piercings.** Turn the blank over and use a compass or circle template to draw a line around the outside of the openings created by the four chips you removed. Shave down the curved chip walls using the line as a guide to make sure all of the pierced cuts are the same size.

5 **Carve the small chips in the center.** When working on a new pattern, it can be helpful to mark the chips to remove. Then, carve the four small three-sided chips (see page 8) in the center to create a positive diamond design.

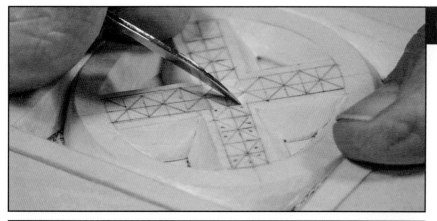

6 **Turn the diamond into a cross design.** Place the blade just to the right of the center on one side of the diamond. Make a shallow cut extending from the edge to the center of the diamond. Move your hand into Position 2 with the cutting knife (see page 5). Make a second cut that meets the first cut in the center. Chip carvers call this a "flip-flop cut." Remove the two-sided chip and repeat both cuts on the other three sides of the diamond.

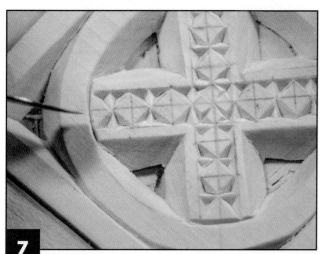

7 **Carve the crosses on the legs of the X.** Use the same procedure as in Steps 5 and 6. Start in the center and work toward the ends. When carving adjacent chips, make the first cut on the second chip with the knife blade pointing away from the already-carved chip. This prevents the side pressure exerted by the blade from damaging the wall between the two chips. Then, cut the two-sided line chips around the edges of the legs of the X.

8 **Carve the border.** To finish the ornament, carve two-sided chips (see page 8) around the ring. You may have drawn the lines on the blank if you used the layout method on page 11, but you can also carve the lines freehand if desired.

Variations

You can alter all of the patterns in this book to create your own unique carvings. There are lots of different ways to use the same pattern to carve a different ornament—for example, you can add chips, leave chips uncarved, remove chips altogether, or split a chip into smaller chips. Or you can change design elements entirely to create your own pattern. You can also use other tools, such as nail sets, gouges, or a scroll saw, to add texture, relieve areas, or cut out chips. Choose larger chips for these variations; any chip that you can pierce can also be relieved, textured, or cut out.

In the examples below, I used tools, modified design elements, and carved chips to create different triangular configurations. If you follow the layout method outlined on page 11, you'll see how you can carve different chips to create different designs—in the original pattern, I carved crosses on the arms of the X, not triangles, but I can still use that pattern to carve triangles on the arms of the X by choosing different chips to remove.

In the relieved version, I added a simple line border, carved three-sided chips to change the center embellishment, and cut three-sided chips on the arms of the X to make triangles that point toward the center. In the textured version, I segmented the border with line cuts, cut triangles that rotate 90° from each other for the center embellishment, and cut three-sided chips on the arms of the X to create triangles that point away from the center. In the scrolled version, I didn't add any borders and focused on the center and arms of the X. I cut eight three-sided chips in the center to create a star shape, cut three-sided chips to create diamond shapes on the arms of the X, and added small three-sided chips around the edges of each diamond.

Relieving

If you'd like to relieve areas of an ornament, make a stop cut around the outside of the area, about 1⁄16" (2mm) deep. Then, use a 1⁄8" (3mm) mini gouge to remove the top layer of wood. The goal is to evenly remove the wood up to, but not beyond, the stop cut.

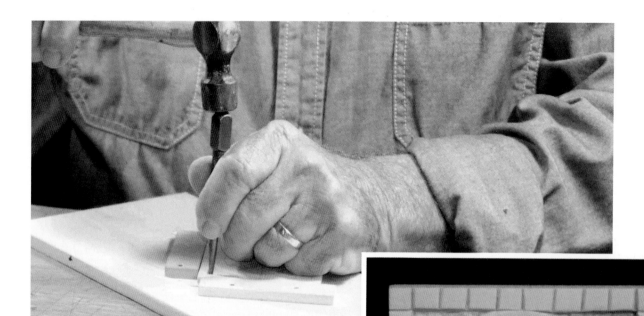

Texturing

There are tools made specifically for texturing carvings, but I use a nail set. Nail sets come in various sizes. The end of mine measures about 1/16" (2mm) in diameter. A diameter that's too small will create holes in the wood instead of small round dimples. A light hammer, such as a tack hammer, is easier to control to achieve an even force when hitting the nail set.

Scrolling

If you have access to a scroll saw, you can cut out sections of your ornament to create a totally different look.

Finishing

Some chip-carved ornaments look better with a natural finish, while others benefit from some pops of color! Judy and I felt that the ornament used in the carving and variation instructions was better left natural, so we chose a floral-themed ornament to illustrate our painting technique. Every ornament is different, so decide what feels best for the ornament you're currently carving.

Natural Finish

Erase any remaining layout lines, and sand the ornament lightly with 220-grit sandpaper. Use an old toothbrush to remove any dust in the chips. Make sure all of the lines are removed; they'll be impossible to remove after you apply the finish. Do not sand so much that the ridges between the chips lose their crisp edges. Apply a clear spray finish. Allow the finish to dry, and then examine the carving to make any final adjustments. When you are satisfied, sand lightly and apply another coat of clear spray finish.

Adding Color

If you plan to add color, alter the finishing process slightly. After you sand and remove any dust, apply a light coat of clear spray finish to both sides, and apply a heavier coat to the end grain. The goal is to seal the surface, especially the end grain that absorbs finish quickly, without adding so much finish that the paint will not adhere properly. Allow the finish to dry, and lightly sand the ornament with a worn piece of 220-grit sandpaper. Then, use a new piece of 220-grit sandpaper in a sanding block to smooth the end grain. The clear finish stiffens the grain, which makes it easier to sand the end grain smooth.

We use water-soluble wax crayons thinned with painter's flow medium to add color to our carvings because the crayon and flow medium mix provides color without covering the wood grain. The crayons are also compact and easy to use on the go, and you don't have to remove the colors from the palette when you're done; all you have to clean up is the flow medium. The colors will be ready to use for your next painting session!

To hang any ornament, drill a hole through the face or the side (depending on the design) or insert a screw eye into the top.

1 **Prepare the colors.** Scribble with the crayon on the bottom of a palette cup to apply a layer of color. Put a small amount of flow medium in another palette cup.

2 **Applying the color.** Wet a #5 round brush with flow medium, and draw the brush through the crayon material to load the brush with color. Apply a light coat of the color to the carved chip. Apply additional coats to build up the intensity of the color.

Play with colors to create a different look for each ornament!

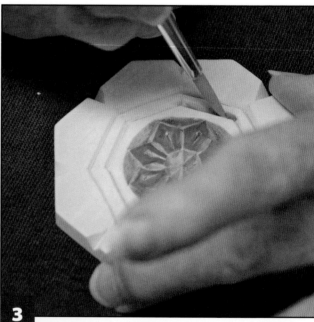

3 **Adding details.** When painting the narrow chips on the outside of the ornament, keep a damp rag handy to remove any paint from the uncarved areas. Allow the paint to dry for at least 12 hours before applying a coat of clear spray finish.

Note: Finished pattern is on page 19.

Patterns

----------------- *Stab marks*

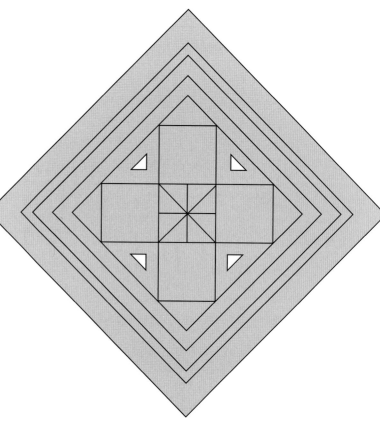

------------------ *Stab marks*

---------------- *Stab marks*

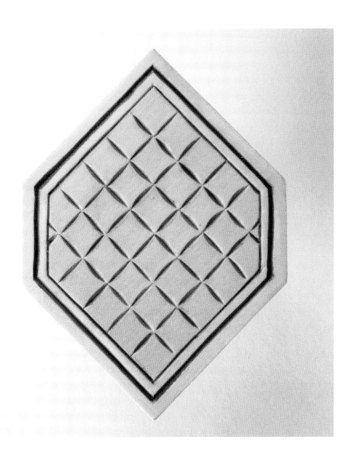

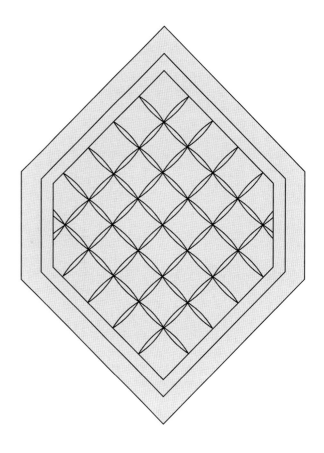

---------------- *Stab marks*

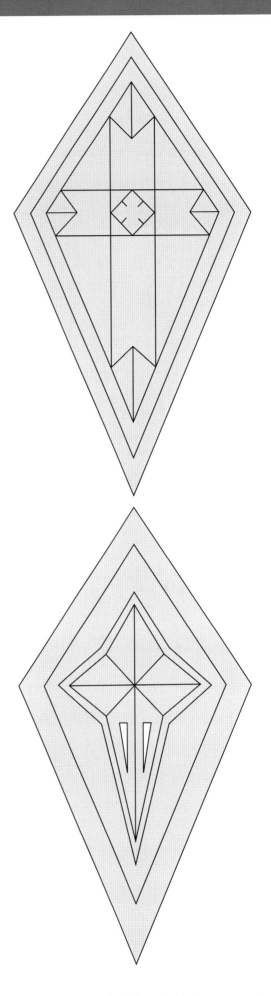

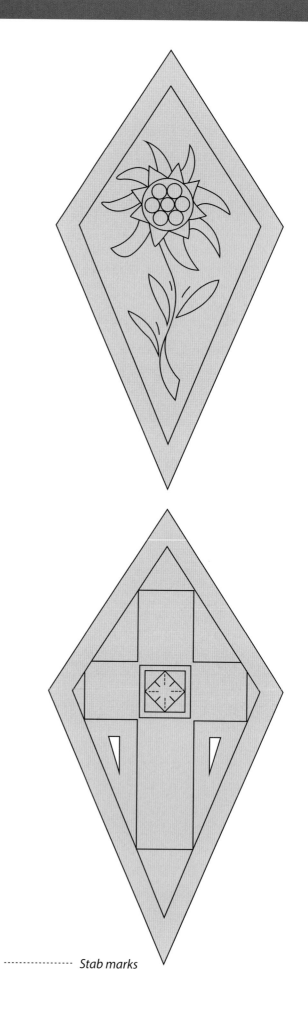

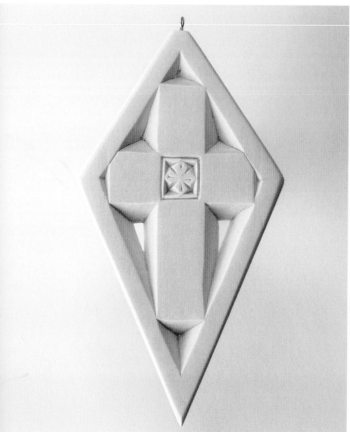

----------------- *Stab marks*

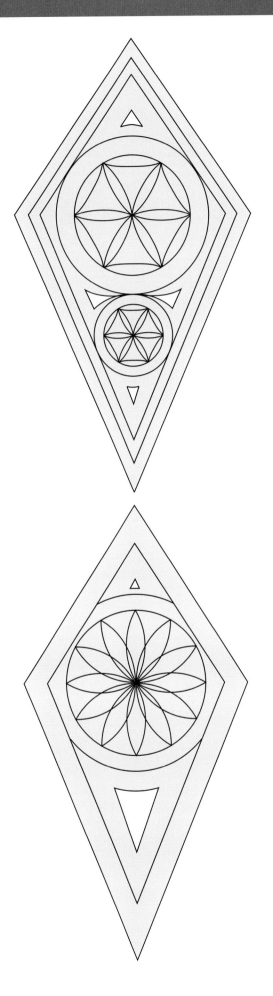

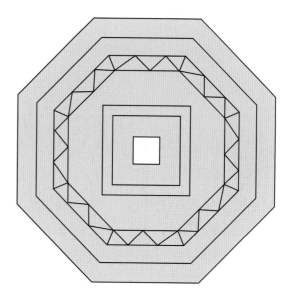

-------------------- *Stab marks*

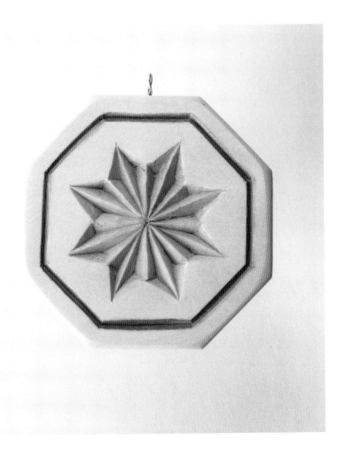

Stab marks

-------------- *Stab marks*

-------------- *Stab marks*

Chip Carved Christmas Ornaments   **47**

Resources

These are a few of our favorite resources, but feel free to explore retailers near you. For the most up-to-date information on retailers, check out an issue of *Woodcarving Illustrated* or go to www.WoodcarvingIllustrated.com.

Alpine School of Woodcarving Ltd.
Wayne Barton
225 Vine Ave.
Park Ridge, IL 60068
wayne.barton@comcast.net
847-692-2822

Heinecke Wood Products
Tim, Robyn, and Ben Heinecke
137 27½ Ave.
Cumberland, WI 54829
dale@heineckewood.com
715-822-3524

John Dunkle Knives
jcdblades@gmail.com
419-494-5948

Nicholas Woodcarving Ltd.
Bruce and Judy Nicholas
nicholaswoodcarving.com
bjnicholas@earthlink.net
937-214-0775